INVISIBLE

PROFESSIONAL

TO

INFLUENTIAL

LEADER

25 Leadership Tips for Women Leaders Who Are
Ready to Lead Authentically with Confidence

BY AUTHOR AND EXPERT

LISA ANDERSON

SPHR, SHRM-SCP, CPC

*Hope you enjoy the tips in this book!
Stay positive and keep shining!*

Lisa Anderson

ISBN: 978-0-578-76708-6

Printed in the USA

Foreword

I met Lisa Anderson about fifteen years ago through an interview process for an HR Director position. I was in an HR Vice President position, and we were looking for a strong HR Director for one of our largest and most complex business units. Getting to know Lisa, I recognized a positive person, technically competent, and someone eager to advance in her career. This interview process led to her hire, and our long-standing relationship as manager, colleague, mentor, and friend.

A good part of our time working together was spent in support of a rapidly growing company, heavily involved in mergers and acquisitions. Together, we supported many integration activities and we learned adaptability – the quality of being able to adjust to new conditions. In the space of just a few years, we became experts at strategically transforming HR and merging work cultures. It was not always easy. Challenges, teamwork, and creative solutions converged to help develop us into the confident and purposeful leaders we are today.

Lisa has a passion for supporting women leaders, helping them find their leadership voice, increasing executive presence, and building leadership courage. In this collection of leadership tips, Lisa presents everyday scenarios and shares her own experiences. She reflects on what she learned from me – but more importantly – it is what I have learned from her, and what you can learn too. Have you ever been afraid to speak up at a meeting, or wondered how to build trust and credibility? Maybe you have encountered a bully along the way? Do you know your values? Lisa tackles real life leadership situations and suggests workable solutions. She teaches us not only the importance of our actions but also why we should reflect and learn from our successes and failures.

A few years ago, I wrote a letter of recommendation for Lisa. Here is an excerpt from my commendation. My thoughts then remain relevant today:

Lisa is a person of strong character. She is self-disciplined and has an amazingly positive attitude. She brings together a rare combination of leadership ability, technical Human Resources (HR) knowledge, strong ethics, and superb communication skills. She knows herself well as demonstrated by her confidence in delivering excellent performance in every role. She is a natural leader with strong resolve and a commitment to continuous learning demonstrated through her own personal education, including her advanced degree, as well as her commitment to share learning with others.

Enjoy this book!

Find your leadership voice. Develop executive presence. Build leadership courage.

Ilene Colina, SHRM SCP

Human Resources Executive
Albuquerque, New Mexico

Dedication

This book is dedicated to any woman leader who has ever felt invisible at the proverbial leadership table. I wrote this book to let you know that there is a light at the end of the tunnel and it's not a speeding train. I was once that leader who didn't feel confident in expressing my leadership voice. I felt like an invisible professional. My hope is that you can utilize the tips, complete the action & reflection exercises, and come out stronger and more confident to transform from an invisible professional to an influential leader.

Acknowledgements

I've been blessed with being born to amazing parents and an extended family that has always supported me. The older I get and the more experiences that I have, I know this to be true. My family is a strong support system for me and I'm grateful for them. ***Mom and Dad, I love both of you immensely.*** It's too many family members to name, the Clayborne and Taylor families are the salt of the earth.

To my husband Frank. You've been there for me. Thanks for your understanding and support the many nights that I have come home from a full-time job, eaten dinner, and retreated to my office. I know you were wondering what was going on in that office, all you could see was the back of the chair and the smoke coming from the computer. Thanks for your patience as I pursue my dreams. I love you.

To my girls, my inner circle. We've been there for each other as we journey through this thing call life. From our college days at JMU to thirty years later, we are still there encouraging each other and lifting each other up through the ups and downs. I love and appreciate you all**, *Liz, Felicia, Karen & Dara*.**

To Dr. Cheryl Wood – the amazing Master Speaker Coach. It was in your Speaker Development lab where you said:

"write the book". I remember your exact words, "you have years of experience, write the darn tip book." You opened my eyes to the possibility of writing my first book and to get over the fear and the intimidation thinking my first book had to be a novel. I heard you Dr. Wood, and I appreciate the work that you do to uplift women and help them get their story into the world. So, finally, here's the tip book.

To Dr. Marilyn Porter, my book coach/editor. Thank you for your support as you encountered a person that had hit a brick wall with her writing. You helped me get back on track and over the hurdle to get this book finished. I appreciate your prayers and your guidance to assist me with this book.

To Tanisha Mackin, my publisher. Thank you for saving the day with this book project. You brought calmness and empathy to a chaotic stressful situation. I am forever grateful.

To Ilene Colina, my former boss, mentor, and friend. Ilene, you hired me into an organization with a lot of change (at the time). You had the confidence in me to lead an HR team for the region. I saw you in action and I learned how to build credibility with grace and dignity. You saw something in me and your hiring decision was instrumental for my career. In that organization, I was able to move up the ranks to a Vice President position. As I reflect back, we also had some good times. Over the years, I've always said, I'm going to write a book because we can't make this stuff up, well, here's the book.

To everyone who had a hand in making this book project become a reality, thank you. For anyone that I may have missed, please charge it to my head and not my heart.

Love you all,

Lisa

The journey begins …

Early in my career, when I was a new manager, I felt I had a good control of my department and the HR expertise that I brought to the table. I realized if I wanted to make a big impact, I had to interact with other departments and become a valuable asset to the organization. In that area, I struggled. My confidence was not always there like it was when I was dealing strictly with HR. Sometimes in meetings I would feel invisible. I would sit quiet and not contribute. It's not that I didn't have anything to say, I just wasn't confident in putting my point of view out there. I thought I was going to be judged, what if it wasn't the right answer? So instead of taking that risk, I would say nothing.

I really had to dig deep and take a step back and address why I felt invisible in these situations. Yes, the fear of judgment was part of it, but another part was the fear of not being liked by everyone. If I had a different opinion than the majority, I was afraid that they (the majority) would look at me and say, "Oh boy, HR is blocking us or causing roadblocks." For some reason, I was taking that very personal.

I also had a huge fear of failure or making a mistake. A survey by the social network Linkagoal found that **fear** of **failure** plagued 31% of 1,083 adult respondents — a larger **percentage** than those who feared spiders (30%), being home alone (9%) or even the paranormal (15%). This tells me I'm not alone. For me, the fear was so paralyzing that I would not take risks or stand confident in my decisions because what if my decisions were not the right decisions. When I think back over my career, the mistakes and the failures are what got me to where I am today. My perspective changed. I look at the mistakes as a part of my development and growth because I'm always learning.

To overcome this fear, I decided to get to know my clients on a 1 on 1 basis. The more I worked with the employees and managers, learning their business and their challenges, the more they got to know me. They saw that I did have something important to contribute. Once I felt comfortable with people in a 1 on 1 situation, it became easier for me to speak up in meetings because those individuals knew me, and I knew them. I was no longer afraid of the judgment because the employees and managers knew I was coming from a place of helping and supporting. They also realized that I really knew my stuff from the HR perspective and I really could help. I started receiving more invitations to meetings where they wanted the HR voice (my voice) in the room.

I went to a new company where I had a great example of an HR Leader in my boss. She had this way about her, and all of the senior leadership respected her. She managed in a collaborative way and when she pushed back, it was in a respectful way. She offered alternative solutions to get to the same result. What I learned from her was that as HR professionals, our job is to be a consultant and let management know the risks and consequences of business decisions from the people's perspective. At the end of the day, the leadership had the final decision (unless there was illegal behavior/activity, which she would escalate straight to the top). What I learned from her was how to operate with grace, dignity, and respect. She is one of my mentors to this very day.

So, why did I write this book? I wished I had a book like this that I could refer to that talked about some of the intangible things. It's great to have all of the technical knowledge in your chosen field, but that technical knowledge doesn't necessarily show you or tell you how to lead and become a more confident leader. Especially if you've felt invisible coming up the ranks. I hope that you will learn something from each tip, take action and ponder on the reflection exercises. This book is intended to be a living document, as you have different experiences in your career, pick up this book and continue to work through the actions and the reflection questions. See what new things come up for you as you grow in your career.

LEADERSHIP TIPS

Tip #1

Know your values. Get Clear.

It's easier said than done. Often, life gets the best of us and we're running on that hamster wheel at 100 mph. You're going through the motions of life at home and work. Taking a pause and reflecting on my values was an eye-opening experience for me. I always thought I had an idea of what my values were, but I never really took a step back and really evaluate them and why they were important to me. I was able to get clear on my top 5 values. I often conduct my own sanity check to see if the priorities have changed (based on life) and whether my top 5 values have changed. There may be a high value (not top 5) that may shift in priority due to the constant change of life. This new awareness has helped me tremendously when I have run into situations where I have struggled. I can look at the situation, determine what's not in alignment with my value system, and then make a decision or modify my behavior according to my values.

ACTION

Can you list your top 5 values and articulate why they are important to you? If you are not clear on your top values, that's okay, you can do the Values exercise here, or visit my website at www.positivelyinpursuit.com.

Subscribe and receive the FREE values exercise delivered to your inbox.

1. _____

_____

2. _____

_____

3. _____

_____

4. _____

_____

5. _____

_____

VALUES ASSESSMENT

Select your top 5 values based on its importance in your life and your career. Rate each of those values on a scale of 1 to 10 based on its importance in your life/career. Then rate each value on a scale of 1 to 10 based on how well you live each value or "walk the talk."

Value	*Value Rating* 1 to 10	*Action Rating* 1 to 10
Accomplishment		
Abundance		
Achievement		
Adventure		
Altruism		
Autonomy		
Beauty		
Clarity		
Commitment		
Communication		
Community		
Connecting to Others		
Creativity		
Emotional Health		
Environment		
Excellence		
Family		
Flexibility		
Freedom		
Friendship		
Fulfillment		
Fun		
Holistic Living		
Honesty		
Humor		
Integrity		
Intimacy		
Joy		
Leadership		
Loyalty		
Nature		
Openness		
Orderliness		
Personal Growth		
Partnership		
Physical Appearance		
Power		

Positively in Pursuit

Value	Value Rating 1 to 10	Action Rating 1 to 10
Privacy		
Professionalism		
Recognition		
Respect		
Romance		
Security		
Self-Care		
Self-Expression		
Self-Mastery		
Self-Realization		
Sensuality		
Service		
Spirituality		
Trust		
Truth		
Vitality		
Walking the Talk		

REFLECTION

Think about a time where you had a work situation that you struggled with. What was it about the situation that made you uncomfortable?

_____

_____

_____

_____

_____

_____

_____

_____

_____

_____

_____

_____

_____

_____

_____

_____

_____

_____

Identify 1 or 2 things that may not have aligned with your top 5 values.

1. _____

_____

2. _____

_____

How was the situation resolved from your perspective?

_____

_____

_____

_____

_____

_____

Were you satisfied with the resolution? Why or why not?

_____

_____

_____

_____

_____

Tip #2

Growth can get uncomfortable. BE prepared for the discomfort

This tip is for all of the perfectionists of the world, me included. We want everything to be perfect, for me personally, I don't like putting out mess. However, I recognized early on in my career that if I waited to roll out an initiative, or not execute a plan because everything was not in place, until everything was perfect, I would have never accomplished anything! I had to learn to roll with an 80% solution and understand that it was not going to be the end of the world if it wasn't at 100% at the time of the rollout. That was very uncomfortable for me, knowing it wasn't perfect. I've learned to become comfortable with the uncomfortable. Things can be adjusted and tweaked and the 80% was okay. I wasn't compromising quality because the solution was at 80%, so why was I stressed out? I know a lot of people that sit on their brilliance because they are trying to get to a 100% solution. Don't let that be you!

ACTION

List 2 things that you are currently working on that you're not 100% comfortable with.

1. _____
   _____
   _____
   _____
   _____
   _____

2. _____
   _____
   _____
   _____
   _____

What is it about the projects that have you feeling uncomfortable?

_____
_____
_____
_____

Is there an 80% solution and if so, what does that look like?

_____

_____

_____

_____

_____

_____

_____

_____

_____

_____

_____

_____

_____

_____

_____

_____

_____

_____

_____

_____

_____

_____

REFLECTION

What have you been sitting on because you're waiting for a 100% solution?

_____

_____

_____

_____

_____

_____

_____

_____

_____

_____

Have you ever worked on something that has made you very uncomfortable because you knew that it wasn't your best work?

_____

_____

_____

_____

Describe your feelings and where you are (or what happened) with the project?

_____

_____

_____

_____

_____

_____

_____

_____

_____

_____

_____

_____

_____

_____

_____

_____

_____

_____

_____

_____

_____

_____

Tip #3

***Take Action – even when you're scared,
Take Action - even if it's a baby step***

Fear can be a powerful thing. How do I know? From personal experience. I had a whole lot of fear around starting a business. The fear kept me paralyzed for 20 years! I've received support to move through my fears and take action even when I don't know what's going to happen. Entrepreneurship is new to me, hell, I've been in corporate America my entire career. I have found a new joy in learning new things and enjoying the journey (instead of looking to the end and missing all of the juicy nuggets embedded in the journey). So now, I'm taking action even though I'm scared to death and I'm taking action even if it's a baby step. I'm also learning to celebrate the baby steps – which is new for me!

ACTION

How does fear show up for you?

_____

_____

_____

_____

Is there something that you're fearful of that has had an impact on your life?

_____

_____

_____

_____

What support do you think you need to tackle this fear?

_____

_____

_____

_____

REFLECTION

List one thing that you accomplished in spite of your fear?

_____

_____

_____

_____

_____

_____

How did you celebrate that win (overcoming your fear)?

_____

_____

_____

_____

_____

_____

Tip #4

Be 100% Committed

How many of you have ever worked on a project and you were not 100% committed to the project? Maybe you didn't understand why you were doing it OR you just didn't agree with the solution. Bottom line, your heart wasn't in it. What were the results? Maybe the project was completed on time, and it was a huge success, but how did you feel about your contribution to the project? If you're not 100% in agreement with something, and you have to do it anyway (because your boss told you to), how do you get to a point where you can contribute and feel good about it. What if the project did not align with your personal values and morals? Over my career, I have worked on many projects and I didn't agree with the approach or solution. How did I get to a place where I felt okay with moving forward? I told myself that even though I didn't agree with something, the overall project was important to the organization or the employees (and not just me). I had to tell myself sometimes, "Lisa, it's not about you." The good news is that I've never worked on a project or been asked to work on something that violated my personal ethical standards. To become successful as a leader, you need to be clear on what's important to you (back to the values tip) and get clarity about what your company or organization's values, mission and vision to see if there is alignment. You will never be in a good space if you're working on something that doesn't line up with your personal values and morals.

ACTION

What does 100% commitment look like with regards to your career?

_____

_____

_____

_____

_____

_____

_____

_____

_____

_____

_____

_____

_____

_____

_____

_____

REFLECTION

List an initiative that you were 100% committed to and had passion towards it.

_____

_____

_____

_____

_____

_____

_____

_____

_____

_____

_____

_____

_____

_____

_____

_____

What were the behaviors and characteristics you exhibited while working on that initiative?

1. _____

_____

2. _____

_____

3. _____

_____

4. _____

_____

5. _____

_____

<u>*Tip #5*</u>

Believe in what you're doing.

Why did you choose your career field?

What is your why?

There are so many women that are going through the motions without honing in on their why.

"I chose the field of Human Resources because I believe that everyone deserves to be treated with respect and dignity in the workplace, no matter who you are. I get to make a direct impact on that for the employee and the organization. If we (as employees) are going to spend an enormous time at work, I want to make sure that the environment is one that warrants growth, creativity, and civility."

From a personal perspective, when I was growing up, I always felt that I needed to help others, stand up for someone that I didn't think was treated fairly. I have contributed those experiences directly to why I chose the career field that I'm in. That is my why. For me, when I think of my why it motivates me on the tough days and keeps me working towards making an impact, even if it's in just one person's life. So, again I ask: What is your why? Do you believe in what you're doing and achieving in your career?

ACTION

Write down your why. Why did you choose your career field? What keeps you going every single day? Your motivation may have nothing to do with your professional life, it can be personal.

REFLECTION

What significant event(s) in your life had an impact on why you chose your career? It doesn't have to be big thing, it can be something small that had a great influence on your "why."

Tip #6

Ignore the Naysayers.

This is something that I wished someone had told me early on in my career. Unfortunately, there is always someone that doesn't want you to get ahead OR they don't care for you and you don't know why. People are people and it's not your job to figure out the underlying intentions of someone else. The only person that you can control is YOU (your reactions, your behavior, your attitude). Have you ever heard the saying "kill them with kindness"?

A "naysayer" is different than a bully. The dictionary's (Merriam-Webster) definition of a naysayer is a person who criticizes, objects to, or opposes something or someone. According to the Workplace Bullying Institute (WBI), a bully is repeated, health-harming mistreatment of one or more persons (the targets) by one or more perpetrators. It is **abusive conduct** that is:

- Threatening, humiliating, or intimidating, or
- Work interference — sabotage — which prevents work from getting done, or

- Verbal abuse

These are two very different definitions. This tip is about ignoring the naysayer. However, if you find yourself the target of a bully, there's a different course of action. If you're being bullied, try to get out of the situation by going to a trusted advisor within or outside of the organization. The key is to get help. If your manager (unless he/she is the bully), your HR department, the Legal department is not willing to take action, you may need to turn to external forces for support to get the bullying behavior to stop. If you are the victim of a bully, remember these things:

B - Believe in yourself. There is no excuse for

bullying behavior. Believe that you're worth not being treated in a disrespectful manner. No matter who it is doing the bullying.

U - Understand that the bullying behavior is the

bully's issue. There is nothing you have done to warrant the behavior.

L - Look to get out of the situation by soliciting help (confidant, HR, manager, Employee Assistance Program (EAP).

L - List all of the behaviors/treatment that you have endured. Document the information so that you may articulate the facts clearly when describing the bully's behavior towards you.

Y - Yield to not letting the bully get away with the behavior for one additional minute. Stand up and seek assistance. Do not try to do it on your own, find a strong support system that can help you get out of the situation.

Please follow the advice above if you are dealing with a bully.

If you are working with a naysayer, ignore the naysayer. Over my career, I have worked with numerous professionals and there were a time or two I may have worked with someone that I didn't particularly care for (professionally) but that person never knew it. Professionalism is one of my top values, so I could work with them in a professional environment all day long with no issues. I didn't have to hang out with them after work or go to happy hour with them. It was a professional relationship and we were able to get our jobs done and meet all of our business objectives.

ACTION

How do you handle workplace naysayers?

_____

_____

_____

_____

What impact has a "naysayer" had on your attitude or your ability to get your job done?

_____

_____

_____

_____

If you are being bullied, take action. Contact your HR representative and share the experiences you are having with the individual(s).

If you're comfortable, report the bullying behavior to a representative of the company (manager, HR, another leader, Legal) so they will have an opportunity to take action. If action is not taken after you've reported it, it's time to look outside of the organization for support. This could be contacting an attorney or if a hostile environment has occurred, filing a claim with the Equal Employment Opportunity Commission (EEOC).

REFLECTION

Have you ever had a "naysayer" push your buttons to the point that you lost control?

_____

_____

_____

_____

_____

_____

_____

What was the situation?

_____

_____

_____

_____

_____

_____

_____

What were the lessons learned from your response to
the situation?

1. _____

   _____

   _____

2. _____

   _____

   _____

3. _____

   _____

   _____

4. _____

   _____

   _____

Tip #7

Don't be afraid to fail; it's called lessons learned.

We all have failed at something. If you're living life, you have failed a time or two. The key is what do you do after you've failed. Do you pick yourself up, brush yourself off, and keep moving? Or do you stay stuck at the point of failure unable to figure out how to move forward? In my personal life, I had a huge fear of failure. When I embarked upon the journey of becoming a certified coach, I had a peer coach that asked me this life-changing question "Lisa, you have had so much success in your professional career, why do you not think you would have success starting your own coaching business?" This question changed my life! I then realized that the fear of failure had stopped me in my tracks when it came to starting my own business. I also had a success coach tell me, "Lisa, you need to fail at least 3 times a day, because as an entrepreneur failure is inevitable and you need to become comfortable with failure." Wow! My mind was blown. I really had to assess my relationship with the idea of failure and shift my mindset. What's your relationship with failure? You could have a relationship with failure that you know it may show up on your doorstep, and if it does, you welcome the experience and look for the juicy lessons learned. Brilliant ideas are born from someone's failures.

ACTION

How do you perceive failure? Is there anything in your career that you perceive as a failure? Share this with a mentor or someone that you trust to gain a different perspective.

REFLECTION

Here or in your journal, write down 2 or 3 recent failures. Analyze the failures (i.e. what went wrong, why do you consider it a failure). What are the lessons learned? What can you do different next time?

1. _____
   _____
   _____
   _____

2. _____
   _____
   _____
   _____

3. _____
   _____
   _____

Tip #8

Building Credibility. Do your homework and know your craft.

What is your expertise?

What is your zone of genius?

Are you a Subject Matter Expert (SME) in your chosen field?

What are you known for?

The answer to all of these questions is important when you're trying to establish credibility. You can be new to a company, where no one knows you, one way to build your credibility is knowing your craft and becoming the "go to" person when it comes to XYZ. I did this early in my career. I loved the field of human resources and I decided that I wanted to learn any and everything about the field. I went for my master's degree in HR, I took classes in various HR topics, I became certified in HR (the certification process was pretty intense), but I was passionate about learning about my chosen career field. Over the years, I gained valuable experiences that added to my

HR knowledge toolkit. Now, being a seasoned professional, I can truly say that I am the "go to" person for employee relations and HR at my organization.

.

ACTION

What activities are you doing TODAY to master your craft? Here are some examples of things that you can do to enhance your craft.

- Continuing education
- Certification in your discipline
- Getting a mentor to work on a specific area
- Picking up projects that will stretch you in the area you would like to grow in
- Joining various networking groups
- Join the local chapter of your professional association
- Volunteering

_____

_____

_____

_____

_____

_____

_____

_____

_____

_____

REFLECTION

Name 2 experiences that you went through that could be added to your knowledge toolkit.

1. _____
   _____
   _____
   _____

2. _____
   _____
   _____
   _____

What was it about those experiences that you believe were so valuable, that it was significant enough to add to your knowledge base?

_____
_____
_____
_____
_____
_____
_____

Tip #9

Find a way to show your value

Before you are able to "show" your value, you have to understand what value you have that you're offering or bringing to the table. As an HR professional, there are so many times where I had to show my value and show that I was there to help not hinder progress. This was important to me because if managers did not see the value in HR, they would go around us or not involve us in their business issues. If employees did not see the value in HR, they would not come to us when they were experiencing a problem.

Often times I am asked whether showing your value means that you have to stab someone in the back or pull someone else down so you can be "seen". So many professionals make that mistake. Every day, you have a unique opportunity to show your value to yourself as well as others and it doesn't always involve waving your hands around trying to get someone's attention. It can be very subtle. Let's say for example, the value you bring to the table is your ability to craft a story around metrics (the numbers). Your colleagues are sitting around a table discussing the next Board Meeting where the metrics will be presented. You are asking powerful questions about the numbers so you can understand the story. Then you turn around and beautifully tell the story behind the numbers. You have not stepped on anyone, you haven't pushed a person to the floor and stepped on their back to shine, but yet, you were able to show your value.

ACTION

What value do you bring to the table?

Is it dependability?

Is it your writing?

Is it your gift of gab?

Identify the value and tell 1 instance of you showing your value to yourself or others.

_____

_____

_____

_____

_____

_____

_____

_____

_____

_____

_____

_____

_____

_____

_____

Reflection

Has there ever been a time where you could have shown your value, but you chose to stay quiet? What was the situation? Why did you decide NOT to show your value? What was the outcome of the situation?

_____

_____

_____

_____

_____

_____

_____

_____

_____

_____

_____

_____

_____

_____

_____

_____

Tip #10

Follow Up & Follow Through

I equate these two terms (follow up & follow through) with execution. There are people who are good at strategizing, drawing out the plan, talking about the big picture, they can talk all day about a project (and they can really have you drinking the Kool-Aid), but then when it comes to execution...it's a big letdown.

They lack follow-up & follow through skills. This can be a big drain on a person's credibility. Some leaders equate these terms with integrity. Meaning, if they said they were going to do something, they follow through and get it done. It's like the saying "my word is bond" and if they don't follow through, they are letting down on their word. Some people don't do well with this because they feel that if they follow up/follow through...they have to have ALL the answers, and because they don't have all of the answers, they will not follow up. In my career (even to this day), I don't have ALL the answers. What my customers know is that if I don't have the answer, I will tell them that by saying I need to conduct more research to find the answer, and then I get back to them. If a day has gone by, and I still don't have the answer, I follow up with them to let them know that I am still working on the research and that I will get back to them by a certain date. At this point, I must follow through. My credibility is on the line and my customer is waiting on an answer so they can make an informed business decision. This is one of the fastest ways to earn respect from your peers, following up and following through on your commitments.

Have you ever worked with a person that did not follow through on their commitments and it directly impacted your ability to get your job done? I have! For someone like me that likes to get things done (yes, I am a self-admitted over-achiever), it drives me absolutely crazy. The way I look at it is my credibility is still on the line even if I have to wait for someone else to get their part done so I can do my part. Follow up and follow through (or the lack thereof) can impact you directly or indirectly and can-do harm to your respect and credibility with others.

ACTION

Let's do an honest assessment.

How is your follow-up/follow through skills? (No one is peeking at your answer).

_____

_____

_____

_____

What have you done this week to follow up/follow through on a work or home related project?

_____

_____

_____

_____

REFLECTION

Have you ever witnessed the lack of follow up/follow through skills with a leader or boss (doesn't have to be YOUR leader/boss)? What were the specific behaviors that the leader exhibited that made them lack in this area? How did the people following the leader feel about their leader's lack of follow-up/follow through skills?

_____

_____

_____

_____

_____

_____

_____

_____

_____

_____

_____

_____

Tip #11

Listen to Others

Believe it or not, many managers and leaders struggle in this area...listening to others. Often they "hear" what people are saying, but they are not "listening" to what people are saying. I have interacted with leaders who while someone is talking, they are busy formulating their response in their heads. When they do respond, you can tell that they were hearing what the other person said, but they were not listening. When I encounter this, I often ask the person, "What did you hear me say?" OR "What is your understanding of what you heard?" This will assist in making sure your message was clearly heard so you can make a decision of whether you need to clarify your overall message.

ACTION

Practice your listening skills. Listen to a podcast (your choice) and highlight the top 3 takeaways from the podcast.

This particular exercise will help you hone in on your listening skills.

Why did I pick a podcast for this exercise? A podcast can have good content, but sometimes depending on the length of the podcast, it's so easy to get distracted by other things (especially if you're multi-tasking in your head). This exercise will help you to stay focus and drown out the distractions.

1. _____

_____

_____

2. _____

_____

_____

3. _____

_____

_____

REFLECTION

Describe a time when you did not do a good job of listening?

_____

_____

_____

_____

_____

What were the implications (i.e. time wasted, project not completed, confusion)?   What was the lesson learned in that situation?

_____

_____

_____

_____

_____

_____

_____

_____

_____

_____

Tip #12

Show courage. Stand up for what is right.

In my HR career, there have been times when I've had to go up against a manager because I felt like we were not doing the right thing when it came to an employee. Especially if I saw a manager treat an employee a certain way (maybe because they didn't like them) or if I felt an employee was being treated unfairly. As an HR professional there is a balance that one must take on, doing what's right for the business but also being an employee advocate. As I moved up the corporate chain into the VP of HR position, there were times when I had to push back to a VP of Operations where we didn't agree. This took leadership courage, something that I have to admit I didn't always have. Leadership courage is like a muscle, you have to work and build it up. I started to feel the shift in my career in my leadership courage when I became very clear about my value system. I always had a motto that if I couldn't sleep at night over a work issue, I needed to go back and address that issue because there was something that didn't sit right with me. I now understand that the work issue didn't feel good because it rubbed against a value that was important to me. Leadership courage can also look like going against the popular vote or against the grain. Everyone may be going right, and you go left. It can sometimes feel lonely. The good news is that there are many organizations that value leadership courage. They value diversity of thought and they don't want people on the team that will always agree. They want people that will speak up when things don't feel right, and they want diverse perspectives. Are you working at that kind of organization?

ACTION

Evaluate your organization's culture.

Are you working at an organization that wants to see leadership courage?

_____

_____

_____

How about your manager/supervisor? Does he/she want you to show leadership courage and stand for what's right?

_____

_____

_____

If the answer is no, how do you operate in that environment?

_____

_____

_____

_____

REFLECTION

Think about a time when you had to exhibit leadership courage. What was it about that situation that made you take pause and speak up or stand for what's right?

Tip #13

Admit mistakes instead of passing the blame or not taking responsibility.

I've seen many leaders over my 25 year career that will not admit they made a mistake. I'm not sure why, they may see this as a weakness. I've also seen leaders that would not take responsibility on things that fell directly in their area of responsibility. They will either blame market conditions, their employees, or the organization, but they will not accept accountability for a mistake. When employees witness this with a leader, they sometimes perceive they can't trust the leader. Making a mistake is okay, we're human beings. What happens after the mistake is where a leader can gain or lose credibility with their employees. In my career, I'm always the first to raise my hand when a mistake is made. I will let someone know that I dropped the ball with an apology. A genuine apology. After that apology, I will tell the person what my plan is to fix the mistake (if it's fixable). If my mistake is not fixable, then I will share with the person what measures I will take to make sure the mistake doesn't happen again. This is not to say the person is happy in the end, but I've expressed my true concern for the impact of my mistake. When I became a leader with my own HR team, I kept with the same standards. My team has made mistakes. The first question I ask team members is "What happened?" I want to hear my team's side of the story. I want to get an analysis of the situation so I can see if a mistake was made on our part. If it is, we go through lessons learned and I apologize on behalf of the team for the mistake AND a here's what we're going to do to fix it. If it's not my team's mistake, I am coming to the table to explain what happened and what we could do to prevent this from happening again. I'm not passing the blame, here are the facts, here is my team's role in it, what can we do to make sure it doesn't happen again. In this situation, I have come up against leaders that wanted to point the finger at my team (again, passing the blame). I have to admit, I have had incidents of being a mommy bear and fighting for my team. I'm not afraid to fight and stand up for my team. It goes both ways, if we make a mistake, I'm the first to admit it. If we didn't make the mistake, and someone comes after my team, I will stand up for my team and fight (professionally). I digress, I'm just keeping it real. We all know that this happens in corporate America. The moral of the story is, don't be afraid to admit to mistakes and at all cost, stay true to yourself in those moments.

I have to admit, it's much easier to admit to mistakes in my professional life than it is in my personal life. In my personal life, some mistakes that I've made had emotions tied to it which made it more difficult to admit to the mistake because someone was going to be hurt. What I've learned is that we are all human and the longer we live, the more mistakes we will make. In my personal life, I am still the first one to raise my hand to admit to a mistake and to deal with the consequences (if any) of my mistake.

ACTION

Take a look at your top 5 values and determine which of those values would have a strong reaction to you making a mistake. Journal about that value and what experiences you've had in the past that lends to the reaction (i.e. childhood experiences, career limiting experiences).

_____

_____

_____

_____

_____

_____

_____

_____

_____

_____

_____

_____

_____

_____

_____

REFLECTION

Think back to a time you made a mistake and there was a huge impact.

_____

_____

_____

_____

_____

_____

How did you handle it?

_____

_____

_____

_____

Were there people negatively impacted because of your mistake?

_____

_____

_____

_____

How did this make you feel?

_____

_____

_____

_____

_____

Tip #14

Increase Your Exposure and Visibility in the Organization

With this tip, you may ask yourself, "How do I increase my exposure and visibility in the organization?" The first question I have for you is "What are you known for in the organization?" Are you known for the quality of your work? Are you known for your expertise in your field? Are you known for your tenacity for delivering and getting the job done? Whatever you're known for, which is hopefully a strength for you, leverage your strength to get exposure in the organization. You can also get assistance with exposure and visibility by letting your manager or supervisor know that you would like to participate on different projects. Another way is to volunteer when new opportunities arise. You can also network within the organization to get to know people (building relationships) and letting them know what your career aspirations are. You never know what other people know and they will remember you when they hear about different opportunities and projects. Exposure and visibility work both ways. Some people get exposure and visibility in a negative way, for things that they don't do well. For example, not pulling their weight on projects, a bad attitude, or not being dependable. Focus on your reputation and what you would like to be known for in the organization.

ACTION

Ask a few people in your organization (that you trust) how they perceive you. Try to get an idea of what you're known for in the organization (by others). Compare those responses to what you would like to be known for. Do they align?

REFLECTION

Think about a time when you had the opportunity to work on a project team or a new initiative in your department, division, or organization. Why do you think you were asked to participate on the team? Journal about the experience and what you gained out of the experience. If you have not had this experience in the workplace, think of other places (i.e. church, volunteering) where you may have worked on an initiative.

_____

_____

_____

_____

_____

_____

_____

_____

_____

_____

_____

_____

_____

Tip #15

Maneuver around the Office Politics

There are many people that are not in leadership to this day because of office politics. They don't want to play the office politics game. The unfortunate thing is that office politics just don't come to managers and leaders. You don't have to be in a management position to find yourself in the middle of office politics. The solution to this is all in the way YOU respond to office politics. This is where your value system should kick in at its strongest. Your values will determine how you respond to office politics. Depending on the organization, the higher up in management or leadership you go, the stronger the office politics can get. In my career, I've managed to maneuver or deal with the office politics head-on. Once I got clear on my values, I was able to respond to office politics in a way that felt good to me. For me, it was important to stay true to myself and to walk in integrity and authenticity. Often times, this meant that other people were not happy because they expected a certain response from me and it didn't happen. Especially those that were deliberately trying to push my buttons.

Early in my career, they received the response they were looking for because I allowed people to push my buttons. With growth and leadership maturity, I was able to overcome that and hone in on who I wanted to be as a leader. In the end, that's the only thing I have total control over...ME and how I respond. It's the same for you. The only thing you have total control over is YOU and how you respond to situations.

ACTION

Describe a situation in your workplace where office politics is at the forefront. Are you involved in it? What is/was your response in the situation?

_____

_____

_____

_____

_____

_____

_____

_____

_____

_____

_____

_____

_____

_____

_____

_____

_____

REFLECTION

Think about the worst office politics situation that you have ever encountered or witnessed.

_____

_____

_____

_____

_____

What was it about the situation that made it so bad?

_____

_____

_____

_____

What was involved in it (i.e. bad leadership, gossip, rumor mills, he said/she said, etc.)?

_____

_____

_____

_____

_____

_____

_____

Tip #16

Find your Voice

This tip is important for women leaders.

Do you have a voice?

Are you comfortable sharing your voice? Do you trust that you CAN share your voice?

As a woman, it can be hard to share our voice in some environments, especially male dominated environments. I have had the experience of being the only female leader on an Executive Team. When I first joined the team, I was quiet in most meetings because I was new, and I was trying to feel out my colleagues and I'm pretty sure they were doing the same with me. I wanted to fit into the team, but I also wanted to show the team that I added value based on my knowledge and expertise. What worked for me was as I started to build relationships with my colleagues, it made it easier for me to share my voice when we came to the table (in a meeting format). Building genuine relationships with my peers made me comfortable and it made them comfortable with me. When I shared my voice, viewpoint, and perspective, they listened and respected what I brought to the conversation. There were many times when I may have disagreed with an approach, but I was able to disagree respectively, lay out the pros and cons of my position, and was still respected for my opinion and perspective. Every environment that I've worked in, I had to find my voice in that environment in order for me to be effective in my role. Have you found your voice in the environment that you're currently working in today? What are you doing to build or strengthen your voice?

ACTION

What is your voice in the environment that you're currently working in?

_____

_____

_____

_____

_____

What are you known for bringing to the "table"?

_____

_____

_____

_____

_____

If I were to ask any of your colleagues about your voice, what would they tell me?

_____

_____

_____

_____

_____

REFLECTION

Think about a situation where you felt like your voice wasn't heard. What was the situation?

_____

_____

_____

_____

Why did you feel like your voice was not heard?

_____

_____

_____

_____

Tip #17

Practice having a strategic mindset.

When I first entered the management ranks, I had a hard time transitioning from thinking about my department to the bigger picture. I was so engaged with what was going on in my HR department, I would miss what was going on around me in the company. I had to intentionally practice being strategic because it wasn't natural for me. This happens to a lot of new managers. One way I was able to overcome this was having an honest conversation with my manager where I told her that I needed to develop a more strategic mindset and that I needed her help. The good news is that she took on the challenge. She started to include me in strategic meetings (where she could) or she would share with me details from strategic meetings so I could ask questions and get a better understanding.

Being in HR, a lot of the initiatives that we were responsible for aligned directly to the strategic operations of the company, so this was very helpful. My manager really helped me to connect the dots. So, if thinking strategically doesn't come natural for you, find a way where you can practice strategic thinking. If you are not able to do this inside of your organization, think about ways outside of your company where you can intentionally develop this area. Just like a muscle, you can work on it (by working out) to strengthen it.

ACTION

Is strategic thinking one of your strengths? If it is not, what can you do to develop this area? List two things you can do to intentionally develop this skill, inside or outside of the organization.

1. _____
   _____
   _____
   _____
   _____

2. _____
   _____
   _____
   _____
   _____

REFLECTION

Think about a time where you were so entrenched in your "lane" (i.e. your department, your group) that you missed the bigger picture. Was there any impact to you missing the big picture?

_____

_____

_____

_____

_____

_____

_____

_____

_____

_____

Tip #18

Increase your Executive (or Leadership) Presence.

What is Executive Presence? Before you can increase it, you have to understand what it is. You sometimes see this in job postings and job descriptions, that one must have "Executive Presence". Often times, it's hard putting executive presence into words, sometimes you just know it when you see it. Leaders with great executive presence have a physical, mental, and emotional presence about them. All of us have witnessed a person who walks into a room and they have this presence about them. You can't quite put your finger on it, but they are able to command a room with just their presence. They have a confidence about them, and they haven't opened their mouth. People are drawn to them. When they are networking, you may see people around them. From a mental perspective, they are a mastery of their craft, they may be an expert in their field and/or they may have a strong business acumen. They are perceived as credible. They may have an ability to connect with people in an authentic way (a high level of emotional intelligence).

I experienced something in my career that I believe the lack of executive presence had an impact on...I did not get a promotion. I was working in a prestigious organization as an HR Manager. The organization decided to bring in a HR Director since it was me (the HR Manager) and the VP, HR. I was hesitant about applying for the HR Director position but then I thought, 'if I don't apply, what is the message that I'm sending to the leadership team, that I don't want to grow and be promoted'. So, I decided to apply.

I interviewed for the position and I didn't get it. I was okay with that, the only thing that I asked of the VP, HR was that they bring someone in that I can learn and grow from. I was very upfront that my career goal was to eventually become an HR Director. Well, the new HR Director was hired and within the first 3 months, I quickly realized that my HR knowledge was stronger than my new boss. That made me angry.

I started to reflect on why I was not selected, and I believe that executive presence had a lot to do with it. To be the HR Director at such a prestigious organization, the organization was looking for a certain presence whic I admit, I did not have at that time in my career. So, what did I do? Remember, I was angry, so I became very intentional. I started to apply to HR Director level positions outside of my current organization to see if I could move to the next level in my career. I was surprised because companies started calling me based on my resume. I then thought, *'I may not be ready to be an HR Director at this organization, but clearly other organizations think I'm ready.'* Within 3 months, I had an offer and I resigned. I went to a new organization as the HR Director. Eventually, I was promoted to VP, HR at that company and was there nine years before the company was sold to another organization. Based on that experience, executive presence is something that I intentionally worked on when I got to my new organization as a Director.

Now that I've shared my experience about the lack of executive presence and I've described some characteristics of executive presence, what are some ways that you can work on increasing your executive presence?

ACTION

Think of people in your workplace or your industry that have great executive presence. What is it about them? If it's someone you know, ask them how they've worked on their executive presence. If it's someone you DO NOT know, introduce yourself and let them know you would like to add them to your network and why.

_____

_____

_____

_____

_____

_____

_____

_____

_____

_____

_____

_____

_____

REFLECTION

There are physical, mental, and emotional components to executive presence. If you were to reflect upon these three areas, how would you rank them from strongest to weakest?

Example:

1) Mental

2) Physical

3) Emotional.

What is the rationale for your ranking?

1. _____

2. _____

3. _____

_____

_____

_____

_____

_____

_____

_____

<u>*Tip # 19*</u>

Learn how to address and deal with conflict.

To be an effective manager, you have to learn how to address AND deal with conflict. In my HR career, I have worked with SO MANY managers that were conflict avoiders. I'm not saying you have to be a lover of conflict, what I'm saying is that you can't avoid it if conflict presents itself. Avoiding it can lead to other things such as loss of credibility (as a manager), retention issues (loss of good people), and overall morale issues with your team. The way to address conflict head on is to try and have an objective attitude when it comes to the conflict (even if the conflict directly involves you). This is where leadership maturity plays big here...sometimes you have to address the conflict without emotion being tied to it (especially if you're emotionally charged about the situation). If you can put a fair balance perspective on the conflict, it makes it a little easier to address, even if you're in the thick of the conflict. I will share one of my favorite HR stories about conflict (it wasn't my favorite at the time it was happening when I found myself in the middle of the conflict).

I was the VP of HR in an organization and I had two high level executives (a female and a male) that could not get along. There were behaviors that were exhibited in front of others (i.e. yelling matches in meetings in front of other subordinate staff) and it made for a very uncomfortable environment. One of my HR team members happen to be in one of the meetings and reported back to me what happened in the meeting. At this point, I had a dilemma.

The behavior was escalating and the mere fact that my team member informed me what had happened, I felt I had an obligation to do something about it. I approached both executives individually to find out what happened and what was going on. This was a sensitive topic because I didn't want them to know that my team member had reported back to me.

The good thing was there were multiple employees in the meeting so I could keep the reporter anonymous. When I approached the female executive and asked her what happened, she started to call the male executive all kinds of expletive names. She supported the male executive but felt that he was an idiot and that he didn't listen to anything she had to say when she was an expert in her area. When

I approached the male executive and asked him what happened, he downplayed it and said that what happened in the meeting was no big deal. He said he disagreed with the approach of the female executive, but at the end of the day, he had to make the final decision and he was accountable for that decision. He discounted it and moved on.

The behavior between the two worsened and more employees were talking in the hallways about their behavior. At this point, something had to change. The female executive had made comments that she was no longer interested in working for the male executive and wanted a move. I tried to make that happen but unfortunately, there were no open positions that would keep her at the same level and rank. She continued to work with the male executive and things continued to progress and became worse. Instead of me trying to figure out what she wanted, I came straight out and asked the female executive what she wanted. She informed me that she did not want to work with this male executive anymore and that she was ready to leave the company to work for someone who appreciated her.

I started working with the female executive to get her a severance package to assist her in her transition. We were able to negotiate a package that she appeared to be happy with. She ended up leaving the organization. Three months later, the organization received a discrimination claim from the EEOC from the female executive. The organization agreed to participate in the mediation process with the female executive. It turned out that the reason she filed an EEOC case was because she felt the male executive was bad mouthing her in the industry. Evidently, she heard from some colleagues in the industry that the male executive was talking bad about her and that could impede her ability to get a job in the industry. Well once we heard that, we immediately put a cease and desist on the male executive. He still worked for us and it was not difficult to speak with him to let him know the impact this action would have for him and the organization. We were able to work out the reference situation with the female executive and she was able to get a positive reference from the organization.

What were the lessons learned in this case?

1) Conflict may arise even in the best of situations

2) No matter the level of the people involved, conflict can still happen (two senior level executives) it's a matter of how you deal with it

3) As the HR person, I felt caught in the middle. I had relationships with both executives, and I was trying to figure out a win/win for everyone.

Sometimes in conflict, there's not a win/win for everyone, someone may be on the short end of the stick. I've learned that you try and figure out what everyone can live with.

ACTION

Are you a conflict avoider?

_____

_____

_____

_____

_____

What was the last conflict situation that you were involved in that you lost sleep behind or you just didn't know how to address it?

_____

_____

_____

_____

_____

What was the situation and how did you handle it?

_____

_____

_____

_____

_____

REFLECTION

The situation you described, think about what were the lessons learned? Reflect upon them here like I did in my scenario.

_____

_____

_____

_____

_____

_____

_____

_____

_____

_____

_____

_____

_____

_____

_____

_____

_____

Tip #20

Get clear about your career goals.

Where are you going in your career? Do you have goals mapped out for yourself? What do you want out of your career? It's easy to wander aimlessly through your career not sure what your goals are. For example, I'm in HR, I've studied and trained to become an HR professional, so it's not like all of a sudden I was going to wake up one day and decide I was going to be a doctor. Even within your chosen industry, there are so many different ways you can take your career. I could have chosen to specialize in a particular area of HR. I could have become a Compensation Specialist or a Training Professional (or several other specializations in HR) but I decided early in my career that I wanted to become an HR Generalist where I get to dabble in all areas of HR. If you have goals mapped out, how are you doing with the goals? Are there action steps that you need to take today to move you one step closer to your goal? It can be overwhelming. Stay focused and deliberate on taking baby steps to move towards your goals. You may think taking baby steps is a small thing, but a small thing is movement. Don't get in a state of complacency and 5 years pass you by with no movement towards your goals.

ACTION

What is the next move or position towards your career goal? List it. If you want some assistance with outlining your career goals, I have a FREE Career Roadmap that can get you thinking about what you want in your career. (Visit my website www.positivelyinpursuit.com)

REFLECTION

What were your last two position moves in your career?

_____

_____

_____

_____

_____

_____

Are these moves critical to you achieving your career goals? Why or Why not?

_____

_____

_____

_____

_____

_____

_____

Tip #21

Effectively Build Genuine Relationships

I have to be honest. As I reflect back over my career, I believe the number one thing that has helped me move up the corporate ladder is my ability to build relationships with people. I have a deep caring for people, and I want to build authentic relationships. Now this is not to say, I walk around happy go lucky wanting to build relationships with everyone. I am not one to try and build relationships with EVERYONE because that is not me and it would not be authentic. However, I do try my best to be open and to be approachable to others. I believe I have earned respect in an organization from people that I don't know based on my reputation of being approachable, open, and fair to others.

So, my question to you...are you building relationships in your organization?

Are they authentic relationships?

Do you struggle in this area?

Be honest with yourself because if this is an area that you struggle with, knowing this about yourself, you can actively work on this. Is it critical for you to build relationships in your line of work and in your career?

ACTION

List two people that you need to build relationships
with personally or professionally?

1. _____

_____

2. _____

_____

Why did you choose these two people?

_____

_____

_____

_____

_____

_____

_____

_____

_____

_____

_____

_____

_____

_____

REFLECTION

What is a critical relationship that you have built and what has been the impact of you having that relationship in your personal life or your career?

_____

_____

_____

_____

_____

_____

_____

_____

_____

_____

_____

_____

_____

_____

_____

_____

_____

Tip #22

Developing Leadership Maturity

I have to set the context for what I mean when I say, "leadership maturity". What I mean by this, is the ability to have maturity when it comes to work related situations and to think what's best for the organization or another person and not necessarily yourself. I didn't know I had leadership maturity until I found myself in the middle of a volatile situation at work that directly involved ME. I was the VP of HR for a division in my company and I was a part of the Sr. Leadership team. Our Sr. Leadership team was a close-knit group, however, our CFO had a reputation of being direct, sometimes loud, and having a quick temper. I knew that our President had great respect for the knowledge that the CFO had. One day I was on my way to work, sitting in traffic, and I was reviewing my blackberry e-mails. Apparently, an argument had ensued on e-mail and an employee had copied me (the VP, HR) into the e-mail string. The employee was upset because he felt that the CFO was calling him a liar on e-mail in front of other people copied on the e-mail. So, I get to work, go to my office and start my daily ritual of getting ready to work (getting my tea, turning on my computer, etc.). The CFO came into my office and we started talking about the e-mail exchange.

I told him that I didn't know the whole story because I was copied in, but my perception was that the CFO was calling the employee a liar on the e-mail in front of others. At this point, the CFO became very angry and he started raising his voice. (If you've ever been in a volatile situation, there's an inside voice that's advising you in real-time as things are happening.) My intuition told me to stop what I was doing and pay attention because he was very angry. I asked him to have a seat so we can discuss the situation because I did not have the history. Well, he escalated. At this point, I put myself in a defensive position just in case he lunged at me. My inside voice was saying, *"Lisa get ready, you may have to take your 3-inch high heel off and beat the hell out of this guy if he lunges at you."* My office door was open, so the entire hallway heard what was going on and stopped moving. His voice went up and then my voice went up.

The next thing I knew, the Executive Assistant to the President came into my office, grabbed his arm, threw him out of my office, and closed my door. Wow! I didn't know what had just happened. I was literally shaking. I had NEVER had that kind of experience in the workplace. I was angry and fired up. I sat at my desk for 5 minutes just to get my heart rate to slow down. My phone rang. It was the President of our Division. He was at the airport getting ready to board a plane and the words on the other end of the phone were "Lisa, are you okay?" I asked him, how he knew what happened and he said his Executive Assistant had called him. I told him that he almost had his VP of HR and his CFO rolling around on the floor because I was getting ready to football tackle this guy. I told him that the CFO's behavior was unacceptable and that I am demanding a meeting with me, him and the CFO when he returned from travel. I hung up. The next call I received was from the VP of Marketing who was at a remote meeting. I answered the phone and he said "Lisa, are you okay?" Well, how did he know...one of his employees on the floor called him concerned for my safety. The next call I received was from the EVP of HR (who I had a dotted line reporting relationship to). I answered the phone and he said "Lisa, are you okay?" and then the second thing he said was "He's fired...how dare he treat one of my HR team members like that...he's out of here." I asked the EVP of HR, to allow me to handle this with him and the President.

After all of the incoming phone calls, I called my husband. I told him what happened and all he could say was "Which police precinct do I need to pick you up at because I know you've been arrested for trying to kill someone?" I told him he would have been proud...but I was angry as hell. Over the next week, me and the CFO did not speak. All of the work that we had to get done, was done through our respective team members. I was angry and I did not want to speak to him until I had the meeting that I wanted with him and the President. Well, that day came. I was able to look the CFO in the face and share with him how he made me feel in those few moments and that the behavior was unacceptable and I wasn't going to take it and no other employee was going to take it anymore. He shared with me and the President some things that he was dealing with in his personal life that may have precipitated the behavior...not an excuse but he wanted us to know. I'm not at liberty to discuss the additional steps that were taken, but believe it or not, after that volatile situation, he and I were able to repair our relationship and continue to work together. When I look back over this situation, where was the leadership maturity? There was maturity when emotions were very high, I didn't have a physical response which would have led to me losing my job and criminal charges. Maturity also showed up when I told my EVP of HR to allow me to handle it with the President. I could have said to him "Yes, let's terminate" but I felt that the situation could be remedied with other measures.

Maturity is that even though that situation was embarrassing for both of us (two Executive level VP's having an exchange like that with other people hearing it), we were able to mend the relationship and I was able to forgive him once I made it crystal clear what my expectations were when he dealt with me or any other employee in the organization.

ACTION

Do you believe you have leadership maturity?

_____

_____

_____

_____

Do you admire another leader for their leadership maturity?

_____

_____

_____

_____

What is it about them that stands out to you?

_____

_____

_____

_____

REFLECTION

Have you ever been in an emotionally charged situation with a co-worker or boss? Were you able to exhibit leadership maturity? If so, in what ways.

_____

_____

_____

_____

_____

_____

_____

_____

_____

_____

_____

_____

_____

_____

_____

_____

#Tip #23

Find a way to become an influencer.

I have to admit, this is easier said than done. However, there are small things that you can do TODAY to work towards becoming an influencer in your organization. This doesn't mean you need to become an influencer with the CEO or the President of the company. You can become an influencer with your boss, your colleagues, your employees, and your customers. This is where people start to trust you as a credible person to the point that they listen to what you have to say, they value your opinion, and they know that you're not just going to tell them what they want to hear. They know that you're going to give them an honest opinion or assessment even if it's not the popular opinion. When you get to the point in your career where you are an influencer, you are invited (and welcomed) to the "table" without having to kick the door down and inviting yourself into the room.

Early in my career, I had to kick the door down to get invited to the table AND I had to do it in a nice way where I didn't tick people off. In the world of HR, sometimes if managers don't value what you bring to the table, they would make decisions without HR. I have even experienced managers going out of their way to make sure HR (me) didn't know about a meeting. Initially, I took this personally, but then I stepped back and asked myself why they didn't want me in the meeting. I had one manager share with me that initially he didn't want me in the meetings because he thought I was going to say "no" to what he wanted to do. I told him we were on the same team and my role was to help him by offering alternative solutions if something was going to go against a policy, rule, or the law. Once he realized that I came to the table with solutions (and not just "no") I started receiving invitations to attend his meetings. I was invited to walk through an open door instead of having to kick the door in.

ACTION

To become an influencer, you have to show why "they" should listen to you.

List one area of your expertise that you could use to become an influencer in that knowledge area.

_____

_____

_____

_____

_____

_____

Why did you choose that area?

_____

_____

_____

_____

_____

_____

What are you known for when it comes to that knowledge area?

_____

_____

_____

_____

_____

_____

_____

_____

_____

_____

_____

_____

_____

_____

_____

_____

_____

_____

REFLECTION

Think of a person in your organization who is viewed as an influencer. What are a few qualities and characteristics that make this person perceived as an influencer?

_____

_____

_____

_____

_____

_____

_____

_____

_____

_____

_____

_____

_____

_____

Tip #24

Assess the impact of your performance

I don't care what role you are currently performing in your organization, the question I have for you is "what impact do you make on the organization, your boss, your employees, your customer, _____ (fill in the blank)?" If you are going through the motions and performing your job at a mediocre level, my advice to you is to find another job. Find a position that's going to motivate you so you can see where you make a direct impact. For example, in my HR positions, I know I made an impact on employees, managers, leadership, customers, and everyone that I come in contact within my role. I understand how what I do everyday touches the lives of many people and I don't take that lightly.

This motivates me to perform at a higher level and to serve people in excellence. What is your impact?

ACTION

How do you make an impact in your role or in the
organization? If you're not able to articulate what
impact you make, you may not be making an impact.

_____

_____

_____

_____

_____

_____

_____

_____

_____

_____

_____

_____

_____

_____

_____

_____

REFLECTION

If you're currently in a role where you feel you are not making an impact, imagine what an impactful role would look like. What are you doing? How are you feeling?

_____

_____

_____

_____

_____

_____

_____

_____

_____

_____

_____

_____

_____

_____

_____

_____

_____

_____

Tip #25

Invest in YOU.

There are many women leaders out there who will invest in themselves. However, there are a group of women that believe that the investment should come from Corporate America or the company/organization that they are working for. Don't get me wrong, yes, organizations should invest in their employees, but if I had waited for an organization to invest in me, I would be way behind the curve in meeting the goals I had set for myself. I realized that I was worth investing in ME. Don't sit back and wait for someone to tap you on the shoulder and tell you that they finally have the budget for you to take a course or a certification class (or whatever it may be). If you can afford to take the class within the time that you want to do it, I encourage you to make the investment in YOU.

Here are some ways that I made the investment in ME. My parents put me through college even though I knew money was tight (I mean they really couldn't afford to send me to school and took out loans to get me through college). I knew I had to graduate in 4 years, no if's, and's, or but's about it. When I made the decision to go for my master's degree, I invested in me and took out loans to get me through (no more parents paying). I worked full-time and went to school part-time to finish my master's degree. When I made the decision to become certified in my field, in this case, the company did make the investment for me to get my certification. The following year, I made the investment and went for the senior certification. A few years ago, I made the investment to attend a coaching certification program.

My company at that time was not in a position to sponsor me in the program. My boss told me that she couldn't pay for it, however, they would allow me the time off to attend the in-person training classes without using my vacation time. I was very thankful for that and I told her that she was investing in me by allowing me to do that. It's time to get creative with investing in yourself.

ACTION

What investments do you need to make in yourself to reach your goals? What are the strategies that would allow you to make the investments instead of holding you back?

_____

_____

_____

_____

_____

_____

_____

_____

_____

_____

_____

_____

_____

_____

_____

REFLECTION

When was the last time you said "yes" to you? It doesn't have to be a course, training, or a certification. What did you say "yes" to? How did you feel about giving yourself permission to say "yes"?

_____

_____

_____

_____

_____

_____

_____

_____

_____

_____

_____

_____

_____

_____

_____

_____

BONUS TIP

Establish your leadership brand.

Your leadership brand is about pulling it all together to establish how you show up in the world. It involves your look, reputation, what you're known for, articulating your voice, credibility, courage, executive/leadership presence, compassion, and any other quality or characteristic that people use to describe you. What are people saying about you when you're not in the room? That's your leadership brand. It doesn't matter what level of leadership you are currently operating at; everyone has a leadership brand. If you are just starting your career, you are establishing your leadership brand. If you are a mid-level leader, you're adding to your leadership brand with how you are managing and leading in the organization. If you are a senior leader, your leadership brand is more than likely established.

ACTION

Do you know what your leadership brand is? If you are comfortable, ask your manager what other managers say about you and the quality of your work. Ask your manager for feedback on your leadership brand.

_____

_____

_____

_____

_____

_____

_____

_____

_____

_____

_____

_____

_____

_____

REFLECTION

Think back to the experiences that you had that helped mold your leadership brand. We all have had "lessons learned" and "teachable moments" that have contributed to our leadership brand.

What are those significant experiences?

1. _____
   _____
   _____

2. _____
   _____
   _____

3. _____
   _____
   _____

4. _____
   _____
   _____

5. _____
   _____
   _____

6. _____

_____

_____

7. _____

_____

_____

8. _____

_____

_____

9. _____

_____

_____

10. _____

_____

_____

_____

BONUS TIP

Managing through Crisis

As I write this last tip, the world has changed. We are in the middle of the biggest health crisis that the world has seen in the past 100 years. The Coronavirus (COVID-19) has rocked our world from what we've known. This pandemic has changed our workplaces by sending everyone home to a shelter-in-place status. Organizations and leaders have had to pivot to a new "normal" with regards to work. Leaders have an entire new set of challenges ranging from managing fully remote teams to having to layoff or furlough their employees. The pandemic has brought upon additional stress with the drastic fast changes to the workplace (I don't think anyone saw this coming this fast), and organizations having to rely on their technical capabilities.

Two weeks before the world stopped, I started a new job. It was a promotional role for me, the Chief Human Resource Officer (CHRO) in a technical organization. This was my next-level and I was so excited to get started. I reported to work at the end of February and was in the office for two weeks before the announcement came for everyone to start working from home. I was just getting to know my new team that I inherited, I was just getting to know the new Executive Leadership team that I was now a part of, and I was just learning where the bathrooms were at the office. Working remotely has forced me to do all of this from home without the in-person connection (I shared with you that connection was one of my top values). Also, now that I was the CHRO at this company, I was responsible for executing strategies to make sure the health/safety of our employees was at the forefront of the organization's priorities.

During this crisis, I was able to see how my new boss led during a crisis (remember, I'm still getting to know him) and I was super impressed. I am fortunate enough to work with a leader that genuinely cares about the employees. The first thing he did was schedule weekly Town Hall meetings every Thursday night at 7:00 pm EST (we have employees in all time zones all over the world) where he gave transparent updates on the status of the company. The second thing he did, which he announced on a leadership call, was to order 13,000 masks from a vendor that the company had done business with that had switched from making widgets to masks to assist with the pandemic. He announced that every employee in the company (approx. 600 employees) was going to receive a fed-ex shipment with 8 to 10 masks to use for their families. When the masks arrived at the office, he and his family (wife and 3 children) along with the Executive Assistant, went to the office and packaged the masks to get them ready for shipment. He announced to the employees at the weekly Town Hall meeting that masks were on the way to their homes. This made me proud. I have the opportunity to work with a leadership team that genuinely cares about the employees. I know this is not the case everywhere, so I definitely consider myself lucky.

ACTION

How has COVID-19 impacted you? What adjustments have you had to make in your leadership style (if any)? What are your challenges?

_____

_____

_____

_____

_____

_____

_____

_____

_____

_____

_____

_____

_____

_____

_____

_____

_____

REFLECTION

With the impact of COVID-19, it has forced a lot of people to step off of the hamster wheel of life and reflect upon what's important. What plans do you have for your career when the pandemic is over? Is there anything that you will do differently?

_____

_____

_____

_____

_____

_____

_____

_____

_____

_____

_____

_____

_____

_____

_____

_____

_____

ABOUT THE AUTHOR

Lisa D. Anderson, SPHR, SHRM-SCP, CPC

Lisa is an HR professional with over 20 years of HR experience. She holds a Bachelor's degree in Management from James Madison University and a Masters' degree in Human Resource Management from Troy State University. She is a Certified Professional Coach through the Institute of Professional Coach Excellence (iPEC). Lisa is also a certified master practitioner in the Energy Leadership Index (ELI).

As a professional Coach/Consultant, I believe in maintaining a positive mindset, creating partnerships with a purpose, and always striving for significant outcomes. Contact me today for an initial consultation, and find out more about how I can tailor my services to your needs.

Visit Lisa's website for more information:

https://www.positivelyinpursuit.com/

Contact:

www.tanishamackin.com

Tanishamackinpublishingllc@gmail.com

Made in the USA
Middletown, DE
23 May 2021